Wait

A journey to discovering the heart of God

Introduction by Cynthia Heald

RUSSELL KELFER

Illustrated by Marianne Richmond

Wait

A journey to discovering the heart of God

To my daughter, Julia, who was so worth the wait … and to her dear namesake, who first gave me this poem when I needed it most. —MR

In loving tribute to my late husband Russell, who was the consummate encourager. —MK

Text Copyright © 2003 Russell Kelfer
Introduction Copyright © 2003 Cynthia Heald
Illustration Copyright © 2003 Marianne Richmond
Book Design by Sara Dare Biscan

Russell Kelfer and Lauren photo Copyright © 1991 Kay Bridges
Lauren photo Copyright © 1991 Kay Bridges
Candle photo Copyright © Paul Liggitt Photography, www.plphoto.com
Adam photo Copyright © 2001 Lynn Schoenstedt
Page 21 sidebar excerpt taken from *The Life God Blesses* by Jim Cymbala
and Stephen W. Sorenson. Copyright © 2001 by Jim Cymbala.
Used by permission of Zondervan.

Scripture quotations are taken from the following versions:
Holy Bible, New International Version (NIV).
Copyright© 1973, 1978, 1984 International Bible Society.
All rights reserved.

Copyright ©2003 Brownlow Corporation
6309 Airport Freeway
Fort Worth, Texas 76117

ISBN: 1-59177-030-0
Printed in the United States of America
Second Printing

The Story of Wait

My dear friend, Julia, gave me this beautiful poem, **Wait,** *in March, 2001, following my third successive miscarriage in a span of nine months. Wishing to comfort me in a time of deep despair, she shared a photocopy with me from a version she'd been given years earlier. "The author?" I asked. "Unknown", she said. I hung it on my fridge for months, then tucked it away as my heart began to heal. About six months later, I was once again talking to God about waiting. (I'm very impatient)! I remembered this poem, took it out of hiding, and re-read it. In that moment, I felt certain that I should pursue finding the author and inquire about illustrating and publishing his or her work. As an author and artist myself, I "just knew" this message could minister to so many waiting for God's direction in their life.*

— MARIANNE RICHMOND

Sometime in the Fall of 2001, our ministry office took a call from a stranger asking to illustrate and publish a poem written by my late husband, Russell. His well-loved poem, **Wait,** *has long circulated on the Internet in that mysterious fashion so common these days — author unknown. Although the petitioner had taken great pains to find the real author of the "anonymous" work, my initial reaction to her request was "No." However, an unseen, restraining hand kept interfering with the delivery of that message. After failing to get even an e-mail addressed correctly, I reached Marianne Richmond by phone.*

When I learned her story and reasons for wanting to do the project, my objections began to slip away. When I was privileged to see her work, the objections disappeared in a great wave of joyful expectation.

Waiting and struggling to keep faith while time drags on is a rather universal condition that presents a need for encouragement. Whatever your personal circumstances, dear reader, may you discover "the treasures of darkness, riches stored in secret places, so that you may know the Lord God of Israel who calls you by name" (Isaiah 45:3). And may you find the joy that it is possible to experience when God's reply to you is "Wait."

— MARTHA WILLIAMS KELFER, WIFE OF LATE AUTHOR, RUSSELL KELFER

Author Russell Lee Kelfer

November 14, 1933 – February 3, 2000

The late Russell Kelfer was an ordinary man who shared an extraordinary relationship with the Lord. The San Antonio businessman had no formal training for the wide teaching ministry to which God called him. His wisdom and insights were learned directly from his study of the Scriptures and his love for Jesus Christ.

His 45-year ministry moved from mentoring underprivileged children to teaching large groups of adults. His greatest satisfaction came from his one-on-one gentle counseling and his interaction with ordinary people.

His enduring legacy — encompassing hundreds of printed lessons, stories, poems, and audio/visual tapes — thrives as Discipleship Tape Ministries, Inc., (DTM), which shares his teachings free-of-charge with countless people around the world.

Today, DTM is carried on as a faith ministry by his wife, Martha, and by those who knew and loved him.

Introduction

In our fast-paced world, waiting has almost become an extinct activity. The new millennium finds us "microwaving" ourselves through life. As our stress levels increase, our ability to slow down and wait diminishes.

Waiting is certainly not a concept we humans would invent, but it is a priceless principle from the heart of God given to us for the ultimate benefit. Note Isaiah 40:31, **"But those who wait on the Lord will find new strength. They will fly high on wings like eagles. They will run and not grow weary. They will walk and not faint."** When we allow the Lord to lead and guide us, when we stay in His presence and watch Him, it is then that we receive strength.

This is the truth that Russell Kelfer communicates in his insightful poem, "Wait." We impatiently demand solutions to our problems, and God often responds by asking us to wait. We are blessed to have a God whose overriding concern is the development of our character and His desire for us to have an intimate knowledge of Himself. Waiting from God's viewpoint is vital to our faith, hope, endurance, and strength.

So it is with wisdom and love that the Master sometimes gently responds to our pleas with "Child, you must wait."

Cynthia Heald

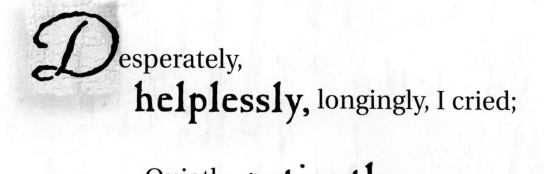

*D*esperately,
helplessly, longingly, I cried;

Quietly, **patiently,**
lovingly, God replied.

I pled and
a clue to

I wept for
my fate....

When I speak at conferences, I frequently have several precious young women tell me they want to do what I do, and they ask how I prepared to be a speaker and writer. When I tell them that for 27 years I washed, cooked, cleaned, and carpooled for our four children before ever beginning a public ministry, they seem a little taken back. These young women are eager to start immediately, waiting, to them, is almost equivalent to wasting time. But as I look back over my life, those 27 years are the foundation upon which I stand. Waiting "in the trenches" taught me more than I could learn from books or teachers. Waiting helped me to see my role as more of a servant, rather than a leader. It was worth the wait.

CYNTHIA HEALD

and the **Master** so gently said,

"Wait."

"**Wait?** you say wait?"
my indignant reply.
"Lord, I need **answers,**
I need to know why!"

Is your hand shortened?
Or have you not **heard?**

Dear Lord,
I so often feel blocked from hearing your voice...

MY FAVORITE PHOTOS

Why. How I feel when I look at them...

By **faith** I have asked, and
I'm claiming your Word.

My **future** and all to which I relate
hangs in the balance,
and you tell me to **Wait?**"

I'm **needing** a 'yes,'
a go-ahead sign.
Or **even** a 'no,'
to which I'll resign.

Ask and it will be given to you; seek and you will find; knock and the door will be opened to you

You **promised**, dear Lord,
that if we believe,
We need but **to ask**,
and we shall receive.

For everyone who asks receives; he who seeks finds; and to him who knocks, the door will be opened.

MATTHEW 7:7-8

Lord, I've been asking,
and **this is my cry:**

I'm weary of asking!

I need a reply.

"*This* is what the Lord says: 'In the time of my favor I will answer you, and in the day of salvation I will help you.'" (Isaiah 49:8) Isn't this a wonderful promise? In no uncertain terms, God affirms that He will answer and will help his people. But notice carefully the time slot for His help and answers: "In the time of my favor … and in the day of salvation." God has a designated time when His promise will be fulfilled and the prayer will be answered. It is a "day" or moment that He knows is best for the help to arrive and the deliverance to be accomplished. His answer is absolutely sure for those who trust Him, but it is not yet.

Herein lies the battle of faith — to hold on and keep believing God despite what our natural senses tell us. Our challenge is to wait in faith for the day of God's favor and salvation.

JIM CYMBALA

Then **quietly,** softly, I learned of my fate,
as my Master replied again, **"Wait."**
So I slumped in my chair, **defeated** and taut,
and grumbled to God,

"So, I'm waiting…

**for
what?"**

I look up to the mountains—does my help come from there? My help comes from the LORD, who made the heavens and the earth! He will not let you stumble and fall; the one who watches over you will not sleep. Indeed, he who watches over Israel never tires and never sleeps. The LORD himself watches over you! The LORD stands beside you as your protective shade. The sun will not hurt you by day, nor the moon at night. The LORD keeps you from all evil and preserves your life. The LORD keeps watch over you as you come and go, both now and forever.

PSALM 121

He **seemed then** to kneel, and His eyes
met with mine . . . and He tenderly said
"I could give you a **sign.**

I could **shake the heavens** and
darken the sun. I could raise the dead
and **cause mountains to run.**

I could give all you seek
and
pleased you would be.

You'd have what
but
you **wouldn't**

you want,

know Me.

You'd not know
the **depth** of My love
for each saint.

You'd not know

the **power** that I give

to the faint.

You'd not learn **to see**
      through clouds of despair;
you'd not learn **to trust**
      just by knowing I'm there.

You'd not **know the joy**
      of resting in Me
when **darkness and silence**
      are all you can see.

We knew you, our precious child, were out there. At night I sat in the glider in the decorated nursery, lit by the globe nightlight, and I spoke to God, and I waited. I knew in my heart God was preparing us for our future child, and the timing was His, not ours.

He was preparing our hearts to put our child first. He was preparing our lives to slow down and create space for a new focus. He was filling me with creativity and inspiration to create the nursery. He was adding to our lives the support system of friends and family to welcome the child. He was touching the heart of the birth mother to choose adoption and to fulfill her adoption plan.

The call came on my cell phone. "Your daughter is being born in Chicago!" the voice said. "Can you come and meet her NOW??" Our dreams were fulfilled. Our daughter found us just two days before her birth through her birth mother's call to our adoption attorney, listed in the local phone book. God is big and the wait is the journey to discovering His heart.

BETSY, MOTHER OF SARAH

You'd never **experience**
the fullness of love
when the peace of **My spirit**
descends like a dove.

You would **know** that I give,
and I save, for a start,
But you'd **not** know the depth
of the **beat of My heart.**

The **glow of My comfort**
late into the night,
the **faith that I give**
when you walk without sight.

The **depth** that's beyond
getting just what you ask
From **an infinite** God who
makes what you have **last.**

You'd never **know** should
your pain quickly flee,
what it means that My grace
is sufficient **for thee.**

And he said unto me, My grace is sufficient for thee: for my strength is made perfect in weakness. Most gladly therefore will I rather glory in my infirmities, that the power of Christ may rest upon me.

II CORINTHIANS 12:9

Yes, your dearest dreams
overnight would come true,
but, oh, **the loss,** if you missed
what I'm doing in you.

So, **be silent,** my child,
and in time you will see
that the **greatest** of gifts
is to
**truly
know
me.**

When I met my husband John, he was passionate about life, music and God. But after we married, he pursued a finance career that left little time for us, music or God. Over time, I slowly watched his heart die.

We nearly lost our marriage, and then John unexpectedly lost his job. We finally cried out to God, "Where are you? What should we do?" God said, "wait."

Over the next two years, we waited. With little income, God provided — just what we needed — while John returned to music. As we waited, we learned to depend on God and seek His desire for our lives. I saw John's passion re-ignite and our faith deepen.

One day, a phone call came. A pastor had heard John lead worship and asked him to become the worship leader at his small church. John said "yes."

Today, that church has grown, and John touches lives weekly with God's word and music. Our marriage is stronger than ever. The joy and passion are back. And we don't ever intend to live life again without God.

Thank you, God. We're so glad you told us to wait.

JULIA

And **though** oft My answers seem terribly **late,** My most **precious answer** of all is still...

"Wait."

To share your stories of waiting with others:
Go to www.waitpoem.com

**To learn more about Discipleship Tape Ministries, Inc. the ministry of
Martha Kelfer and the late Russell Kelfer, please contact:**
Discipleship Tape Ministries, Inc.
10602 Mossbank
San Antonio, TX 78230
(800) 375-7778
www.dtm.org

*"For the past 20 years, our goal is to help pastors, teachers, missionaries,
and other Christians obtain practical materials on spiritual growth."*

To learn more about Marianne Richmond products:
Marianne Richmond Studios, Inc.
420 N. Fifth Street, Suite 840
Minneapolis, MN 55401
(800) 768-9197
www.mariannerichmond.com